Generational Curses: The Bible Cure

By Curry R. Blake

General Overseer
John G. Lake Ministries
and
Dominion Life
International Apostolic Church

Copyright © 2016 by Curry R. Blake
All Rights Reserved

Published by
CHRISTIAN REALITY BOOKS
P.O. Box 742947
Dallas TX 75374
1-888-293-6591

Unless otherwise noted, all Scripture quotations are taken from the King James Bible.

This book or parts thereof may not be reproduced in any form without express written permission of Curry Blake.

Printed in the United States of America.

DEDICATION

I am dedicating this book concerning the truth about generational curses to a friend who was too quickly removed from earth. Prophet Kobus Van Rensburg was an extremely generous soul. His easygoing, gentle nature still inspires me today. He was constantly aware of the "great cloud of witnesses" of which he is now a part. Few passing's have affected me in my soul as much as his did. Though our friendship lasted only a few years, there was instantly and definitely that connection of spirit that happens when two people that truly love God meet.

In ministry you can have lots of "contacts", but few friends. He was a friend to me and I hope he recognized me as his friend.

TABLE OF CONTENTS

INTRODUCTION 1

CHAPTER 1: WHAT DOES GOD SAY ABOUT YOU? 3

CHAPTER 2: WHAT DOES THE BIBLE SAY ABOUT GENERATIONAL CURSES? 19

CHAPTER 3: WHERE DO THESE PROBLEMS COME FROM? 41

CHAPTER 4: WHAT DO I DO NOW? 73

Introduction

Generational Curses as a topic of discussion has risen to new heights in the last few years. Many people come to me from around the world to be set free from various physical sicknesses and diseases. Most often, they have already been prayed for by other well meaning, but misinformed, people. They come to me because the others could not help them. When the others cannot produce results they begin telling the afflicted one that it must be that there is a "hidden" sin or that their problems stem from a "generational curse". When a person cannot produce results, they often revert to putting the "failure" onto the sick person. That does not represent Jesus or His great love and power.

In this book I have endeavored to give clear, concise, and biblical answers to the questions that arise when the topic of generational curses arise. The premise from which I work is simple: The Bible is the inerrant Word of God and it is to be believed exactly as it is written. It is to be obeyed regardless of personal preference. I believe that the information in this book will be used by God to truly "set the captives free".

Introduction

Over the past 15 years many of the ministries that specialize in "spiritual roots of diseases" and "generational curses", have referred their "clients" to us for help when they could not help them. On several occasions, even their staff and leadership have come to us for personal help. We have had the privilege of seeing Jesus set these, as well as many others, free. I believe you will receive freedom and help as you read this book, believe the scriptural truths presented, and put them into action

Chapter 1:
What Does God Say About You?

God has said a lot about you. As a matter of fact, almost everything He said about Jesus, He has said about you.

He has said that you are blessed, healed, delivered, regenerated, justified, sanctified, perfected... and the list goes on and on.

As followers of Jesus, we really have only one task. That is simply to believe what God has said.

John 6:28-29
28 Then said they unto him, What shall we do, that we might work the works of God?
29 Jesus answered and said unto them, <u>This is the work of God</u>, that ye believe on him whom he hath sent. KJV

When you truly "believe on him...", your actions will line up with what you say you believe.

Let me say it another way. You can clean up the outside and still not be clean on the inside, but you cannot clean up the inside without the outside following suit.
As believers, we must decide to choose to believe what the Bible says even when what we see says something

else. We must also decide to believe what the Bible says even when we are told something different by well-meaning "Christians".

So let's settle some things right from the beginning.

First, let's get our terminology and definitions right.

I will be working from the basic premise that everyone reading this is "saved". What do I mean by "saved"?
There is a Bible definition of "saved" and "salvation" and there are other common definitions used by "church people".

The generic definition used by "church people" is: "to have eternal life and go to heaven when one dies".

The Bible definition is much more specific: NT:4982 sozo (sode'-zo); from a primary sos (contraction for obsolete saoz, "safe"); to save, i.e. deliver or protect (literally or figuratively): KJV - heal, preserve, save (self), do well, be (make) whole.

I can be saved from sickness and disease.
I can be saved from sin.
I can be saved from addictions.

For some reason people seem to believe that they can be saved and yet still live in sin. If that were true, what were they actually saved from?

The Bible says that Jesus came to save us "from" our sins, not save us "in" our sins. People need to realize that the wages of sin is still death. God wants us to walk in righteousness and not in unrighteousness, which is sin.

It is like the parent that tells their child not to walk in the street, because if they do eventually they will get hit by a car. It's not that the parent doesn't want their child to "have fun walking". They want them to walk where they will be safe. It's not safe to walk in sin. Sin kills. Sin is bondage.

God has said that you are blessed. (Ephesians 1:3) God has NOT said that you are cursed. The enemy (satan) will try to convince you that God has condemned you. Satan will try to convince you that the problems you experience are God's will.

God has been trying to convince you that He loves you and has paid the full price for you to be free from all the work of the enemy. The enemy, on the other hand, will try to convince you that the bad things you experience are actually God's way of making you a better person, or that they are punishment for things you've done.

While it is true that some of what you experience is called "sowing and reaping", we must also remember that whatever we experience, whatever "bad" things we go through, God is able AND willing to turn those things for our good, IF we love Him and our hearts are set on fulfilling His will for us.

The following verse has been misquoted and used out of context so often that many people actually quote it wrong and as a result "believe it wrong".

Let's look at it and read it exactly for what it says:

Romans 8:28-32
28 And we know that all things work together for good to them that love God, to them who are the called according to his purpose.
29 For whom he did foreknow, he also did predestinate to be conformed to the image of his Son, that he might be the firstborn among many brethren.
30 Moreover whom he did predestinate, them he also called: and whom he called, them he also justified: and whom he justified, them he also glorified.
31 What shall we then say to these things? If God be for us, who can be against us?

32 He that spared not his own Son, but delivered him up for us all, how shall he not with him also freely give us all things? KJV

Verse 28 tells us that everything works together for good for the people that love God and are called by God to fulfill His purpose. This is not referring to people that have what is usually called a "calling". It is talking about people that have answered God call to become followers of His Son, Jesus. (We must also remember that the true context of this verse is about praying, specifically, praying in the Spirit. Verse 26 and 27 speak about the Spirit making intercession for us according to the will of God.)

Verse 29 tells us who the people are that are being spoken about in verse 28. It shows us that God foreknew us and if He foreknew us, He predestinated to be conformed to the image of His Son, for the purpose that Jesus might be the first (born) of many brethren. God's purpose is to produce a vast family of people that are just like His Son Jesus. It is important to note here that this is the true Bible doctrine of "predestination". Bible predestination is to be predestined to be like Jesus.

Verse 30 tells us that if we were predestined to be conformed to the image of Christ, we were also "called" and if we were called we were also justified and if we were justified we were also glorified.

So you see, it is either all or nothing. God has blessed us with every spiritual blessing in heavenly places (Ephesians 1:3). Some of those blessings include "predestination" to look like Jesus. Another blessing is being "called" which simply means to be invited to be saved.

Another blessing which we have received is called "justification". To be justified means to be considered and treated by God just-as-if-I'd-never-sinned. That's an easy way to remember the outcome of justification. Justification in this verse actually means: *Justification - NT:1344 - dikaioo (dik-ah-yo'-o); from NT:1342; to render (i.e. show or regard as) just or innocent:*

So you can see that God's opinion of you is NOT that you are some dirty dog trying to slip into heaven. God's Himself has caused you (with your permission – which you gave Him when you made Jesus your Lord) to be placed into a category that classifies you as called, justified, glorified and predestined to be conformed to the image of Christ.

Everything God is doing is geared toward helping you look more and more like Jesus on the outside, because He has already recreated you to look and actually BE like Jesus on the inside. Glory to God! This means that God is not working against you. He's not trying to make life hard on you. (Believe me, if God wanted your life to be hard, it would be God-sized hard.) God is trying to work with you to make your life a trophy to Him. He wants to use you to show the world how He can turn someone like you around and make them and their life an example of His handiwork.

Before we actually get into the scriptures concerning "generational curses", I want to show you what God thinks about you and where you fit into His plan and will.

The reason that I'm showing you this is because I want you to realize that if God thinks about me the way the Word of God says He does, then there is no way that the things people have told me about Him could be true.

Remember, the following verses are about every person that accepts Jesus as their Lord and enter into the family of God.

Ephesians 1:3-11
3 Blessed be the God and Father of our Lord Jesus Christ, who hath blessed us with all spiritual blessings in heavenly places in Christ: KJV

In verse 3 we see that God hath (past tense) blessed us. We also see that He "has already" blessed us with all (not some – ALL) spiritual blessings in heavenly places in Christ. The word "blessed" here literally means "to speak well of". It is from the Greek word that we get the word "eulogy" from.

A eulogy is a word spoken at a person's funeral. It is when someone says good things about the person that has died. This is a perfect picture of what is being said here. The minute you accept Jesus as your substitute. The minute you accept his substitution for you on the cross, you are counted as "dead". The apostle Paul said, in

Galatians 2:20
I am crucified with Christ: nevertheless I live; yet not I, but Christ liveth in me: and the life which I now live in the flesh I live by the faith of the Son of God, who loved me, and gave himself for me. KJV

He is saying that when Christ died on the cross, He took my place, so that it is counted by God that I died on that cross and I am therefore dead and it is Christ that is now living His life through me. You had to "die" on that cross. To get into the family of God you had to die.

The minute you "died" (accepted Christ's substitute), God said good things about you at your "eulogy". As a matter of fact, according to Ephesians 1:3, not only did God say good things about you, He said EVERY GOOD THING ABOUT YOU THAT HE COULD POSSIBLY SAY! (That is the literal meaning of Ephesians 1:3)

It is important to notice that everything God said about you is true, and that it is about who you are "IN CHRIST". Not who you were, or what you did it is who you ARE IN CHRIST. God has spoken about you and put to your account EVERY GOOD THING THAT IS IN CHRIST. God is reproducing Christ in you, so He spoke everything He could say about Christ, over you, and INTO you.

You might be tempted to say, "But what was true about Christ isn't true about me." Before you disagree with God (which is never a smart thing to do), remember this: God spoke everything that exists into existence. Before He spoke, it did not exist.

When He spoke, it came into being, instantly. That's a really good thing about God. The second He speaks, it becomes. So before you were born-again, none of the things that were in Christ were in you. But the second, you were born-again, God went through the list of everything that was in Christ, speaking them over you, blessing you with every spiritual blessing that is IN Christ. Every good thing in Christ (and I might add that everything in Christ IS GOOD!) is now in you.

The objective of every real Christian is to have their mind renewed so that their mind will agree with what God has placed in their spirit when they got born-again. When your mind and your spirit agree, you will see true life transformation. (Romans 12:2)

Now let's get back to Ephesians...

4 According as he hath chosen us in him before the foundation of the world, that we should be holy and without blame before him in love:

This verse goes along with Romans 8:28 I mentioned earlier, showing God's plan for us that started even before the world started. It also tells us that He chose that we should be holy and without blame.

5 Having predestinated us unto the adoption of children by Jesus Christ to himself, according to the good pleasure of his will,

Once again we see that He predestined us to be adopted as children and that our adoption was according to the pleasure of His Will. Our adoption was His idea and it brought Him pleasure. You, being God's son or daughter, actually brings Him pleasure and is His Will!

6 To the praise of the glory of his grace, wherein he hath made us accepted in the beloved.

Verse 6 is a great verse to memorize, as is every other verse.

In verse 6 we see that our being made accepted in the family actually causes God's grace to be glorified. The fact that He can remove our sins and re-create us in His image shows the greatness of God's ability, but it also shows us even more the greatness of His grace. The fact that He was willing (and able) to change us from fallen creatures to redeemed new creations is so amazing that we will spend eternity getting to truly understand it.

7 In whom we have redemption through his blood, the forgiveness of sins, according to the riches of his grace;

In this verse we again see the reference to God's grace in the sense that His grace is what allowed us to have redemption through the blood. Too often we move so quickly into the things of the Spirit concerning power and gifts, etc. and we forget where we have come from.

We must never forget that the forgiveness of sins, being born into God's family and made clean, is the most important of all heavenly blessings. It is indeed the forgiveness of sin that allows all the other blessings to become ours.

8 Wherein he hath abounded toward us in all wisdom and prudence;

Verse 8 explains that it was through the riches of His grace that has abundantly provided us with ALL wisdom and good judgment.

9 Having made known unto us the mystery of his will, according to his good pleasure which he hath purposed in himself:

We have this wisdom and good judgment because His grace has made what was a mystery concerning His will, known to us. We are to know the will of God. God desires us to know His will.

10 That in the dispensation of the fulness of times he might gather together in one all things in Christ, both which are in heaven, and which are on earth; even in him:

The will of God was that when everything was ready and the time was right, He would gather together a family in Christ. When Christ was sent, it wasn't the end of the world. There would still be people being born into God's kingdom even after Jesus was crucified and resurrected.

Therefore Jesus' work and victory had to have both a working in the past (to make things right) and a continuous working, so that those that believed after the work of the cross was finished, might also get in on the result of that work. This is one way in which the Word of God is alive. The Word of God is continually speaking. To God, Who is the Great I AM, it is always NOW. Whatever He ever was, He will ever BE!

11 In whom also we have obtained an inheritance, being predestinated according to the purpose of him who worketh all things after the counsel of his own will:

Finally, in verse 11 we see what we have in Christ. We have an inheritance.

We have an inheritance because we are heirs of God. Not only are we heirs of God, but we are also joint-heirs with Christ Jesus. (Romans 8:17) God has made us (created us in a way that allows us) to be partakers of this inheritance that God has for the saints (Colossians 1:12-14).

We are heirs of God. We get our inheritance from God. We are joint heirs with Jesus. That means that whatever He gets, we get. Jesus shares His inheritance with all of us who are "in Him".

Remember, I am bringing all this up so that you can get a basic picture of God's opinion of you and so that you can see that He is not handing out curses to His people.

It really comes down to this:

You either have to believe the love God has for you or you believe that God is still mad at you and you have to earn your salvation.

There is NO middle ground.

You must believe the Bible and what it says or believe what some person has said.

You must either believe you are blessed (as God says) or you believe that you are cursed (as some person says).

Now let's see what the Bible says about generational curses.

What Does God Say About You?

Chapter 2:
What Does The
Bible Say About Generational Curses?

Numbers 23:8
How shall I curse, whom God hath not cursed? or how shall I defy, whom the LORD hath not defied? KJV

This verse is not specifically speaking about generational curses, but it does show God's attitude toward curses.

In the following scriptures you will see that there is a progressive revelation of God's heart toward man.

We must always remember that the basis of grace is God's justice.

Because God is just, He had to extend grace or no flesh could live.

If God's basic nature were not just, He would not have needed to extend grace to mankind.

We know that God progressively revealed Himself (and His nature and character) to man over the years. We can see that progressive revelation even in the text of the "Old Testament".

In Exodus 20:3-6 and Exodus 34:6-10, God says almost the exact same thing each time. (Compare verses 5 and 7.)

Exodus 20:3-6
3 Thou shalt have no other gods before me.
4 Thou shalt not make unto thee any graven image, or any likeness of any thing that is in heaven above, or that is in the earth beneath, or that is in the water under the earth:
5 Thou shalt not bow down thyself to them, nor serve them: for I the LORD thy God am a jealous God, <u>visiting the iniquity of the fathers</u> <u>upon the children unto the third and fourth generation</u> <u>of them that</u> <u>hate me;</u>
6 And shewing mercy unto thousands of them that love me, and keep my commandments. KJV

Exodus 34:6-10
6 And the LORD passed by before him, and proclaimed, The LORD, The LORD God, merciful and gracious, longsuffering, and abundant in goodness and truth,
7 Keeping mercy for thousands, forgiving iniquity and transgression and sin, and that will by no means clear the guilty; <u>visiting the iniquity of the fathers upon the children, and upon the children's children, unto the third and to the fourth generation.</u>

8 And Moses made haste, and bowed his head toward the earth, and worshipped.

9 And he said, If now I have found grace in thy sight, O Lord, let my Lord, I pray thee, go among us; for it is a stiffnecked people; and pardon our iniquity and our sin, and take us for thine inheritance.

10 And he said, Behold, I make a covenant: before all thy people I will do marvels, such as have not been done in all the earth, nor in any nation: and all the people among which thou art shall see the work of the LORD: for it is a terrible thing that I will do with thee. KJV

Notice in each passage that it says that the iniquities of the fathers shall pass down to the 3rd and 4th generation. Dr. Sumrall showed us how each generation bridges to 5 generations.

Most people can remember their parents and their grandparents and will live to impact their children and their grandchildren. If you count each generation listed, you will see it spans five generations. So in essence, each person in a family will be impacted by the two previous generations and impact two generations following them.

This shows how a family trait or practice can be passed through five generations.

In the following passage (Numbers 14:16-24) we see the statement again that the iniquity of the fathers (note it is plural denoting the fathers of fathers) shall "visit" the children down to the third and fourth generation. Also remember that Numbers is after Exodus, showing a progression.

Another aspect which is seldom mentioned in typical "generational curse" teaching is that each time after telling of the visiting of iniquities of the fathers upon the children, it also says that God is quick to forgive and shows mercy.

The reason that it is left out is because if they included it, the people would repent right then and the "curse" would end and the generational curse teachers would not have anything left to teach.

Numbers 14:16-24
16 Because the LORD was not able to bring this people into the land which he sware unto them, therefore he hath slain them in the wilderness.
17 And now, I beseech thee, let the power of my Lord be great, according as thou hast spoken, saying,
18 The LORD is longsuffering, and of great mercy, forgiving iniquity and transgression, and by no means

Generational Curses

clearing the guilty, <u>visiting the iniquity of the fathers upon the children unto the third and fourth generation.</u>
19 Pardon, I beseech thee, the iniquity of this people according unto the greatness of thy mercy, and as thou hast forgiven this people, from Egypt even until now.
20 And the LORD said, I have pardoned according to thy word:
21 But as truly as I live, all the earth shall be filled with the glory of the LORD.
22 Because all those men which have seen my glory, and my miracles, which I did in Egypt and in the wilderness, and have tempted me now these ten times, and have not hearkened to my voice;
23 Surely they shall not see the land which I sware unto their fathers, neither shall any of them that provoked me see it:
24 But my servant Caleb, because he had another spirit with him, and hath followed me fully, him will I bring into the land whereinto he went; and his seed shall possess it. KJV

In the next passage, notice how similar it is to Exodus 20:3-6 and notice especially verse 10, where God is telling them that He shows mercy to thousands. Notice also that Deuteronomy is after Exodus in the Old Testament, again, progressive revelation.

Deuteronomy 5:7-10 (Compare to Exodus 20:3-6)
7 Thou shalt have none other gods before me.
8 Thou shalt not make thee any graven image, or any likeness of any thing that is in heaven above, or that is in the earth beneath, or that is in the waters beneath the earth:
9 Thou shalt not bow down thyself unto them, nor serve them: for I the LORD thy God am a jealous God, visiting the iniquity of the fathers upon the children unto the third and fourth generation of them that hate me,
10 And shewing mercy unto thousands of them that love me and keep my commandments. KJV

Now let's get to THE MOST IMPORTANT Old Testament passage concerning generational curses. (Do I need to mention again the fact of PROGRESSIVE REVELATION?) Just in case… Ezekiel is AFTER Exodus, Numbers, and Deuteronomy!

Each time, God increases the revelation that He shares with us concerning His nature and will.

Ezekiel 18:1-32
1 The word of the LORD came unto me again, saying,
2 What mean ye, that ye use this proverb concerning the land of Israel, saying, <u>The fathers have eaten sour grapes, and the children's teeth are set on edge?</u>

(Verse two above is a reference to the general idea of generational curses.)

3 As I live, saith the Lord GOD, ye shall not have occasion any more to use this proverb in Israel.

Here, God says (in a stern voice), NEVER USE THIS AGAIN!

We can see that He is setting the stage for further revelation concerning "generational curses", but one thing is clear… NO ONE WAS EVER TO SAY THAT THE CHILDREN SUFFER BECAUSE OF THE SINS OF THE FATHER AS THOUGH IT IS THE WAY THINGS ARE SUPPOSED TO BE!

Then He begins to give the clearest revelation yet concerning "generational curses".

4 Behold, all souls are mine; as the soul of the father, so also the soul of the son is mine: <u>the soul that sinneth, it shall die</u>.

In this verse He (God) is making it clear that the soul that sins shall die because of it's own sins and not the sins of someone else.

You will need to follow along closely as we look at each of the following scriptures.

5 But if a man be just, and do that which is lawful and right,

In verse four, God said, "the soul that sins shall die."
In verse five we are given an explanation and shown the contrast between "the soul that sinneth" (which must die) and what happens if a man is just and does what is "lawful and right". In the following verses (6-9) we are given the definition of what is "lawful and right". We also see that if he does right, he shall surely live!

6 And hath not eaten upon the mountains, neither hath lifted up his eyes to the idols of the house of Israel, neither hath defiled his neighbour's wife, neither hath come near to a menstruous woman,
7 And hath not oppressed any, but hath restored to the debtor his pledge, hath spoiled none by violence, hath given his bread to the hungry, and hath covered the naked with a garment;
8 He that hath not given forth upon usury, neither hath taken any increase, that hath withdrawn his hand from iniquity, hath executed true judgment between man and man,

9 Hath walked in my statutes, and hath kept my judgments, to deal truly; he is just, <u>he shall surely live, saith the Lord GOD</u>.

From the previous verses we know that if a man does "right", he shall live. (Note: We will look at what "right" is, a little later in the book.)

Now let's see what happens if a "just" man produces a son that is not just…(Which also shows us that a good person can produce a bad person, meaning that every person chooses for himself or herself how they will live.)

The "badness" of the bad son is not the result of a bad lineage through the father.

10 If he (the just man) *beget a son that is a robber, a shedder of blood, and that doeth the like to any one of these things,*
11 And that doeth not any of those duties, but even hath eaten upon the mountains, and defiled his neighbour's wife,
12 Hath oppressed the poor and needy, hath spoiled by violence, hath not restored the pledge, and hath lifted up his eyes to the idols, hath committed abomination,
13 Hath given forth upon usury, and hath taken increase: shall he then live? he shall not live: he hath done all

these abominations; he shall surely die; his blood shall be upon him.

The bad son, (that did not follow in the footsteps of his "just" father) WILL NOT LIVE! HE SHALL SURELY DIE! HIS BLOOD SHALL BE UPON HIM!

His death will be the result of his actions not the actions of his father.

Now let's look at what happens when the "bad son" produces a son that sees his father's sins and DECIDES NOT to follow in his father's footsteps, but rather decides to live right.

14 Now, lo, if he beget a son, that seeth all his father's sins which he hath done, and considereth, and doeth not such like,
15 That hath not eaten upon the mountains, neither hath lifted up his eyes to the idols of the house of Israel, hath not defiled his neighbour's wife,
16 Neither hath oppressed any, hath not withholden the pledge, neither hath spoiled by violence, but hath given his bread to the hungry, and hath covered the naked with a garment,
17 That hath taken off his hand from the poor, that hath not received usury nor increase, hath executed my judgments, hath walked in my statutes;

he shall not die for the iniquity of his father, he shall surely live.

Notice in the above scriptures, God said, that if the son of a bad person decides to walk in God's statutes and not follow the iniquity of his bad father, HE WILL NOT DIE, HE SHALL SURELY LIVE!

God states in the next verse that …as for the "bad father", he will pay for his sins.

18 As for his father, because he cruelly oppressed, spoiled his brother by violence, and did that which is not good among his people, lo, even he shall die in his iniquity.

Apparently the Jews of Ezekiel's day did not like it that God was changing things. They even argued with Him by saying what is recorded in the next verse…

19 Yet say ye, Why? doth not the son bear the iniquity of the father? When the son hath done that which is lawful and right, and hath kept all my statutes, and hath done them, he shall surely live.

They were astonished, they said, "Wait a minute, doesn't the son bear the results of his father's sins?"

To which God reiterated…

"NO!" The soul that sins dies, but the one that lives righteously shall live. The wickedness of the wicked shall be upon the wicked, but the righteousness of the righteous shall be upon the righteous.

20 The soul that sinneth, it shall die. <u>The son shall not bear the iniquity of the father, neither shall the father bear the iniquity of the son: the righteousness of the righteous shall be upon him, and the wickedness of the wicked shall be upon him.</u>

In the following verses, God shows that His desire IS NOT the death of the wicked, but rather that the wicked should turn from his iniquities and do that which is right!

21 But if the wicked will turn from all his sins that he hath committed, and keep all my statutes, and do that which is lawful and right, he shall surely live, he shall not die.
22 All his transgressions that he hath committed, they shall not be mentioned unto him: in his righteousness that he hath done he shall live.
23 Have I any pleasure at all that the wicked should die? saith the Lord GOD: and not that he should return from his ways, and live?

24 But when the righteous turneth away from his righteousness, and committeth iniquity, and doeth according to all the abominations that the wicked man doeth, shall he live? All his righteousness that he hath done shall not be mentioned: in his trespass that he hath trespassed, and in his sin that he hath sinned, in them shall he die.

25 Yet ye say, The way of the Lord is not equal. Hear now, O house of Israel; Is not my way equal? are not your ways unequal?

26 When a righteous man turneth away from his righteousness, and committeth iniquity, and dieth in them; for his iniquity that he hath done shall he die.

27 Again, when the wicked man turneth away from his wickedness that he hath committed, and doeth that which is lawful and right, he shall save his soul alive.

28 Because he considereth, and turneth away from all his transgressions that he hath committed, he shall surely live, he shall not die.

29 Yet saith the house of Israel, The way of the Lord is not equal. O house of Israel, are not my ways equal? are not your ways unequal?

30 Therefore I will judge you, O house of Israel, every one according to his ways, saith the Lord God. Repent, and turn yourselves from all your transgressions; so iniquity shall not be your ruin.

In the next two verses we see the heart of God calling to Israel to turn around. He even tells them that they can have a new heart and a new spirit. He shows them that they can choose to turn and live.

31 Cast away from you all your transgressions, whereby ye have transgressed; and make you a new heart and a new spirit: for why will ye die, O house of Israel?
32 For I have no pleasure in the death of him that dieth, saith the Lord God: wherefore turn yourselves, and live ye. KJV

In verse 31 and 32 above, we see that God was even prophesying what would take place in the New Covenant.

We would be given a new heart and a new spirit. Because of this new heart and spirit (which was not and could not be received by man before the inception of the New Covenant) we are to recognize the work of God in our innermost being. We will talk about the full ramifications of this new heart and spirit and the New Covenant later.

Now let's look at what the New Testament says about "generational curses". Technically, we can't actually look at generational curses in the New Testament, because they are NOT taught in the New Testament. The closest we can get is to look at the mindset that some of Jesus' disciples had.

John 9:1-7 – The Man Born Blind and Generational Curses
1 And as Jesus passed by, he saw a man which was blind from his birth.
2 And his disciples asked him, saying, Master, who did sin, this man, or his parents, that he was born blind?

The disciples were of the belief that apparently all sin or at least all blindness, was caused by sin. They also apparently believed that the sin could be either the sin of the person or the parent's sins.

Some have tried to say that this is proof that the typical doctrine of that day must have been that generational curses were still in effect and since they believed it, then it must be true both for then and now.

Let me say that, No. 1, this passage does not prove that the general population believed any particular doctrine; just that some of the disciples might have believed it.

No. 2, even if they had believed in a particular doctrine, it doesn't mean that the doctrine was correct. Jesus was constantly correcting false doctrines and beliefs among his disciples and the Pharisees and others.

Even in today's vast realm of "Christianity" there are many, many wrong doctrines believed by many people. Just as we have many "flavors" of Christianity today, they had many flavors of Judaism even in Jesus' day. But let's get back to the Scripture passage and see how Jesus responded to the generational curse question His disciples raised.

3 Jesus answered, Neither hath this man sinned, nor his parents: but that the works of God should be made manifest in him.

Jesus said that neither the man NOR his parents had sinned. This kills the idea/teaching that EVERY disease or ailment is caused by a sin. Some sins can cause diseases, but every disease is NOT caused by a particular act of sin. For further proof of this you can also read James 5:14 & 15.

James 5:14-15
14 Is any sick among you? let him call for the elders of the church; and let them pray over him, anointing him with oil in the name of the Lord:
15 And the prayer of faith shall save the sick, and the Lord shall raise him up; and <u>if he have committed sins</u>, they shall be forgiven him. KJV

Notice the word "if" in verse 15. If every sickness or disease were caused by sin, there would be no "if".

Now let's get back to John 9

4 I must work the works of him that sent me, while it is day: the night cometh, when no man can work.
5 As long as I am in the world, I am the light of the world.
6 When he had thus spoken, he spat on the ground, and made clay of the spittle, and he anointed the eyes of the blind man with the clay,
7 And said unto him, Go, wash in the pool of Siloam, (which is by interpretation, Sent.) He went his way therefore, and washed, and came seeing.

Jesus was not saying that the man that was born blind was born blind so that Jesus could heal him. He was saying, IF that man was going to be healed, then He had to heal him while it was day, because night was coming when no one could work. Here He was speaking about His coming death. Once someone (Jesus) dies they can no longer do the work they were sent to do. So all must work while it is "day", while they are alive.

We can clearly see that God does not endorse "generational curse" teaching. He told the Israelites that they would NEVER again say that a father's sins would be put upon the children.

If God is not putting the father's sins upon the children, then what is it that causes the "curses" people see in their lives? We will look at that in the next chapter.

But before we move on, let me take a moment to remind you of what the Scripture clearly states.

People seem to forget that everything we, as ministers of the Gospel, teach, must line up with everything the Bible says. We cannot teach a principle as authoritative in even one area if it contradicts what the Bible says.

Everything we teach must line up with the Bible and everything we teach must line up with everything else we teach.

I can't teach that we are to humble ourselves when talking about character and attitudes and yet claim to have some special anointing that puts me above others. My teaching on the anointing has to match what the Bible says about humility.

All of the Bible must be seamless. There cannot be contradictions or else there will be divisions and strife, etc.

2 Corinthians 5:17-21
17 Therefore if any man be in Christ, he is a <u>new creature</u>: old things are passed away; behold, all things are become new.
18 And all things are of God, who hath reconciled us to himself by Jesus Christ, and hath given to us the ministry of reconciliation;
19 To wit, that God was in Christ, reconciling the world unto himself, not imputing their trespasses unto them; and hath committed unto us the word of reconciliation.
20 Now then we are ambassadors for Christ, as though God did beseech you by us: we pray you in Christ's stead, be ye reconciled to God.
21 For he hath <u>made him to be sin for us</u>, who knew no sin; that we might be made the righteousness of God in him. KJV

If we teach that the person that gets born-again is a new creature and that OLD THINGS have passed away and ALL THINGS HAVE BECOME (present tense) NEW, and that our sins are remitted and God WILL NEVER BRING THEM UP AGAIN. Then we cannot, as God's representatives bring up peoples sins that were part of their old life. This is not to say that if a person is still living in sin that we can't point that out.

Essentially it comes down to this…

You cannot teach the New Birth AND Generational Curses. If you continue to teach both, you will contradict yourself and/or scripture. In Christ, a person is a NEW CREATURE.

One translation says that if any person be "in Christ' they are a NEW SPECIES of BEING THAT NEVER EXISTED BEFORE!

We must realize that when we get born again we get a NEW SPIRIT and a NEW HEART.

When we were translated out of the authority of darkness and into the kingdom of God's Son (Colossians 1:13), we brought nothing of our old spirit across with us. We are now the sons of God. (1 John 3:1& 2)

We are not the sons of the devil any longer. We are not even the sons of our earthly parents any more as far as the spirit goes.

Generational Curses

When you speak of generational curses, you are not speaking of the children of God.

When I got born again, I changed genealogies. My genealogy does not go back to my earthly father or grandfather or great grandfather. My genealogy goes back ONE GENERATION! TO MY HEAVENLY FATHER!

And I have NO generational curses from my Heavenly Father, because Jesus was made a curse for me so that I might be cleansed and become the righteousness of God in Christ. All I have in my genealogy now is generational blessings.

I am blessed with all spiritual blessings in heavenly places in Christ Jesus! (Ephesians 1:3) How can I be blessed and be cursed at the same time? Even Balaam knew that he couldn't curse what God has not cursed.

Beloved God HAS NOT CURSED YOU, HE HAS BLESSED YOU.

I choose to believe what God said about me, rather than what man has taught. Let every man be a liar, but let God be true! (Rom. 3:4)

Obviously, the next question is:

"If it's not a generational curse that's causing all my problems, then what is it?

Now you've asked the right question!

We will cover that in the next chapter.

Chapter 3: Where Do These Problems Come From?

How Do Curses Come?

Proverbs 25:28
28 He that hath no rule over his own spirit is like a city that is broken down, and without walls. KJV

Proverbs 26:1-2
1 As snow in summer, and as rain in harvest, so honour is not seemly for a fool.
2 As the bird by wandering, as the swallow by flying, so the curse causeless shall not come. KJV

In the King James Version of The Bible, punctuation is often less helpful than it could have been.

In the verses above, we see two seemingly unrelated things, yet at a closer look we can see that there is a reason why they may have been put together.

In Proverbs 25: 28 is shows that a person that does not have self-control or discipline is like a city without a wall to protect it. That means anything can just come in anytime it wants and they have no defense.

This aligns with Proverbs 26:1 and 2. It is saying that a person that has no rule over a curse (doom) can come upon a person. The cause is the lack of protection. This ties in with what was said about Job by satan.

Satan said that God had put a hedge around Job that protected him. Satan also told God to "put forth His hand and touch him." Notice God said that satan was the one that would put forth his hand and touch Job.

Job 1:10-12
10 Hast not thou made an hedge about him, and about his house, and about all that he hath on every side? thou hast blessed the work of his hands, and his substance is increased in the land.
11 But put forth thine hand now, and touch all that he hath, and he will curse thee to thy face.
12 And the Lord said unto Satan, Behold, all that he hath is in thy power; only upon himself put not forth thine hand. So Satan went forth from the presence of the Lord. KJV

If you link Proverbs 25:28 with Job 1:10 you will see that they both refer to a wall or hedge of protection.

Notice Job didn't have to really do anything to allow the "curse" to come. When the wall/hedge was removed the enemy could move in. The lack of a wall/hedge was enough to let the enemy in.

In the New Testament we are told to bind or loose, to permit or forbid. We build the wall or remove it. We are told to submit to God AND RESIST the devil and he will flee. We know the enemy goes about as a roaring lion seeking whom he may devour.

He cannot devour anyone or everyone at his will, he has to seek and find those that he MAY devour. He is looking for those that have their wall down. People that have no self-control. People that have no rule over themselves.

God has told us that the Name of the Lord is a strong tower and the righteous run into it and are SAFE!.

Proverbs 18:10
The name of the Lord is a strong tower: the righteous runneth into it, and is safe. KJV

Where Do These Problems Come From?

1 Peter 5:8-9
8 Be sober, be vigilant; because your adversary the devil, as a roaring lion, walketh about, seeking whom he may devour:
9 Whom resist stedfast in the faith, knowing that the same afflictions are accomplished in your brethren that are in the world. KJV

Ecclesiastes 10:8
He that diggeth a pit shall fall into it; and whoso breaketh an hedge, a serpent shall bite him. KJV

Isaiah 5:1-7
1 Now will I sing to my wellbeloved a song of my beloved touching his vineyard. My wellbeloved hath a vineyard in a very fruitful hill:
2 And he fenced it, and gathered out the stones thereof, and planted it with the choicest vine, and built a tower in the midst of it, and also made a winepress therein: and he looked that it should bring forth grapes, and it brought forth wild grapes.
3 And now, O inhabitants of Jerusalem, and men of Judah, judge, I pray you, betwixt me and my vineyard.
4 What could have been done more to my vineyard, that I have not done in it? wherefore, when I looked that it should bring forth grapes, brought it forth wild grapes?

5 And now go to; I will tell you what I will do to my vineyard: I will take away the hedge thereof, and <u>it shall be eaten up</u>; and break down the wall thereof, and <u>it shall be trodden down:</u>
6 And I will lay it waste: it shall not be pruned, nor digged; but there shall come up briers and thorns: I will also command the clouds that they rain no rain upon it.
7 For the vineyard of the Lord of hosts is the house of Israel, and the men of Judah his pleasant plant: and he looked for judgment, but behold oppression; for righteousness, but behold a cry KJV.

Ezekiel 22:30
And I sought for a man among them, that should make up the hedge, and stand in the gap before me for the land, that I should not destroy it: but I found none. KJV

You will notice in all these Scriptures that there is mention of a wall or hedge that is for protection. The lack of that wall or hedge is due to not doing the things necessary to keep yourself strong, disciplined and pro-active.

Words Spoken By Authority:
A spoken curse can only have effect upon you if you believe it. This is why it is so important that parents learn this and speak only blessing upon their children. A

spoken word curse is anything spoken to a child that says that they will not fulfill their God-ordained purpose.

Before, we go further let me show that to you from the Bible.

Mark 11:12-14
12 And on the morrow, when they were come from Bethany, he was hungry:
13 And seeing a fig tree afar off having leaves, he came, if haply he might find any thing thereon: and when he came to it, he found nothing but leaves; for the time of figs was not yet.
14 And Jesus answered and said unto it, No man eat fruit of thee hereafter for ever. And his disciples heard it. KJV

In verse 14 above, Jesus simply said that no man would eat fruit from the fig tree ever again. He did not say something that most people would call a "curse". We know it was a curse because Peter calls it that in verse 21 below.

Mark 11:19-24
19 And when even was come, he went out of the city
20 And in the morning, as they passed by, they saw the fig tree dried up from the roots.

21 And Peter calling to remembrance saith unto him, Master, behold, the fig tree which thou cursedst is withered away.
22 And Jesus answering saith unto them, Have faith in God.
23 For verily I say unto you, That whosoever shall say unto this mountain, Be thou removed, and be thou cast into the sea; and shall not doubt in his heart, but shall believe that those things which he saith shall come to pass; he shall have whatsoever he saith.
24 Therefore I say unto you, What things soever ye desire, when ye pray, believe that ye receive them, and ye shall have them. KJV

Notice that Jesus simply told the fig tree not to fulfill its God-ordained purpose. A fig tree's purpose is to produce figs. Jesus said it would never happen again. The fig tree withered from the roots so as to obey Jesus' command (curse).

This is what happens when a person is "cursed" by their parents by being told that they will "never amount to anything". Their God-ordained purpose is to amount to something. If they believe their parents words they may dry up on the inside and having no root in them, (Mark 4:17) they may try things only to give up when it gets tough.

Or maybe, they were told, "You are just like your father, a no good liar, a drunk, etc." These words will become etched into a child's brain and will form their self- image and become self-fulfilling "prophecies". Jesus said whatever words we speak, and believe will come to pass. Listen to the words your children speak about themselves. If they are speaking doom, if they are speaking defeatist words. Stop them and cause them to change their words. If you change their words, you will change their thinking and you will change their destiny.

James 3:8-10
8 But the tongue can no man tame; it is an unruly evil, full of deadly poison.
9 Therewith <u>bless we God</u>, even the Father; and therewith curse <u>we men</u>, which are made after the similitude of God.
10 Out of the same mouth proceedeth blessing and cursing. My brethren, these things ought not so to be. KJV

NT:2672 – "curse" - kataraomai (kat-ar-ah'-om-ahee); middle voice from NT:2671; to execrate; by analogy, to doom: KJV - curse.

Notice here that it says we "curse" men. This is not the type of curse that people normally speak of when referring to generational curses. This is similar because we are speaking "doom' onto them.

The key is what you do if you hear a person curse you. The average human will curse them back, but we are not average humans, we are the children of God. When someone curses us, we obey the words of Christ and bless them.

Matthew 5:43-46
43 Ye have heard that it hath been said, Thou shalt love thy neighbour, and hate thine enemy.
44 But I say unto you, Love your enemies, bless them that curse you, do good to them that hate you, and pray for them which despitefully use you, and persecute you;
45 That ye may be the children of your Father which is in heaven: for he maketh his sun to rise on the evil and on the good, and sendeth rain on the just and on the unjust.
46 For if ye love them which love you, what reward have ye? do not even the publicans the same? KJV

Most of your problems do not come from what your parents did but from what your parents said and did that you have now picked up and continue to say and do.

Technically, we should not be speaking of generational curses, but rather generational sins. Perhaps your parents had certain mindsets and attitudes towards God and towards sin. Their lives were tainted by those mindsets and the mindsets had actions that went along with them.

As the parents did those actions, they brought certain conditions into your family. If the attitude was a poverty mindset, perhaps the parents were always afraid of losing everything they had or were always worried they would not be able to meet their family's needs.

This mindset would readily be picked up by the children and then they would begin having the same fears. This would cause a chain reaction that would get perpetuated through the family from generation to generation.

Some Christians today would call this a "generational curse", non-Christian people would see it as a low self-image or a self-defeating mindset.

The sad thing is, many Christians today would go to "Christian Counselors" or "Generational Curse Specialists" and spend all their time looking into their family genealogies or trying to find sins that the Bible says have been removed as far as the east is from the west. Non-Christians would set about to correct the mindset through motivational teachings (and would probably make changes for the better).

A few things are certain:

We (as Christians), are never told to look back into our past sinful lives, or into the lives of our ancestors. As a matter of fact, we are told NOT to look back, but to look unto Jesus. As you look at Jesus, meaning looking into who you are in Him, you will see all that God has imparted into you as a new creation. You cannot look at yourself as a new creation and look at your past as though it has anything to do with who you are today.

The apostle Paul said in:

Philippians 3:13-15
13 Brethren, I count not myself to have apprehended: <u>but this one thing I do</u>, forgetting those things which are behind, and <u>reaching forth unto those things which are before</u>,
14 I press toward the mark for the prize of the high calling of God in Christ Jesus.
15 <u>Let us therefore</u>, as many as be perfect, <u>be thus minded</u>: and if in any thing ye be otherwise minded, God shall reveal even this unto you. KJV

It is clear from this passage that Paul did not constantly go back into his past to find the reason for his problems.

He knew the reason for his problems.   satan!

2 Corinthians 12:6-10
6 For though I would desire to glory, I shall not be a fool; for I will say the truth: but now I forbear, lest any man should think of me above that which he seeth me to be, or that he heareth of me.
7 And lest I should be exalted above measure through the abundance of the revelations, there was given to me a thorn in the flesh, <u>the messenger of Satan to buffet me</u>, lest I should be exalted above measure.
8 For this thing I besought the Lord thrice, that it might depart from me.
9 And he said unto me, My grace is sufficient for thee: for my strength is made perfect in weakness. Most gladly therefore will I rather glory in my infirmities, that the power of Christ may rest upon me.
10 Therefore I take pleasure in infirmities, in reproaches, in necessities, in persecutions, in distresses for Christ's sake: for when I am weak, then am I strong. KJV

(Please note: Paul's thorn in the flesh was a messenger (Greek: angelos = angel) of satan. It was not sickness. For proof of this and more in-depth teaching on the subject, see my teaching entitled: "Removing Paul's Thorn".)

Paul knew it was satan that caused his problems, he did not go back into his past and spend time going over the sins for which he was forgiven. God said He would never remember our sins again. So we can only conclude that anyone that brings up our sins is NOT working with God nor representing Him!

Philemon 3:8
Yea doubtless, and I count all things but loss for the excellency of the knowledge of Christ Jesus my Lord: for whom I have suffered the loss of all things, and do count them but dung, that I may win Christ, KJV
Paul made it clear that his past had nothing to do with his present or future in Christ. He said that all the things that he could have boasted about were now counted as dung, as far as he was concerned.

Paul had good reason not to want to remember his past. He had made a career out of hunting down and persecuting Christians. Imagine the memories he had to overcome. Scenes of parents being dragged away from their children, being put into prison to be beat and tortured. Paul had good reason to be the champion of the renewed mind, the champion of Jesus' teaching of what it means to be born-again.

To be a New Creation meant to be free from the past of the old man! It means to be free from the guilt and condemnation that your own mind brings up in memories.

One of the characteristic marks of the New Covenant was that New Covenant Christians were to have their consciences purged of their sins.

Very few Christians that I have met have actually experienced this purging. Paul experienced it to the point that he could talk about the "old man" he used to be and it not affect his position or standing with God. He could actually speak of himself as a trophy of the grace of God, pointing to what God could and did do in a person that counted themselves crucified to the world and the world crucified to them.

Very few Christians even know how to relate to someone that has had their conscience purged. Since they believe they are still the same person they used to be, (the only difference being that God has forgiven them) they are scared to witness or be where sinners are because they think they might fall back into their old ways. Many even still think that God is keeping their sins stored somewhere so that the next time they mess up, all of it will be brought back on them. Very few would actually admit this or say it, but their lives prove they believe it.

John 8:36
If the Son therefore shall make you free, ye shall be free indeed. KJV

Sowing and Reaping:
As we have seen previously, most of the problems normally called curses are simply the result of things that we could have done to protect ourselves and stay safe, but instead we were told they were the result of the past transgressions and iniquities of our ancestors.

One thing should also be noted. If your ancestors ever gave their heart to Christ then their iniquities were washed away and are never to be brought back up. So how are we to deal with them the way many are taught (by going into their ancestor's histories and digging these things back up) and remain true to the Word of God? The truth is YOU CAN'T!

So if it is not our ancestor's past sins that are causing my problems, what is?

It's simple, one major cause of problems in Christian's lives is … Sowing and Reaping

Let me give you the same kind of scenario that God used in Ezekiel.

Let's say Joe was married at an early age and started having children soon after.

As Joe's children grew they saw how Joe did things. They saw his normal everyday life and they saw his weekend drinking binges. Let's say Joe had two sons. Joe was a hard worker during the week (usually). But every now and then, Joe would not only drink and get drunk on the weekend; sometimes he would get so drunk that he couldn't go to work on Mondays. Because of his frequent absences Joe lost his job often. The lack of income and worry "caused" Joe to drink even if it meant spending the food and bill money. He even started gambling so as to try to win back what he spent on alcohol.

This led to frequent moving from one house to a lesser house. Because there would not be enough money to meet the needs of the family, Joe's wife had to hide money from Joe if she wanted to make sure that the children had food and clothing. When Joe found out, he would often get violent, breaking things and even striking his wife.

As stated earlier, Joe had two sons. The older son saw Joe's actions and their results. He vowed to never be like his father. He drew away from Joe and drew closer to his mother. As this son grew older, he started doing what he saw his mother do. He began putting money away in a savings. He seemed to grow up quickly and was exactly the opposite of his father. He became prosperous because he never missed work because he never drank and was seldom sick.

The other son, the youngest, didn't understand what happened; he just knew that his dad was his hero. He wanted to be just like his dad. His dad was a man's man in his eyes. His dad drank, so he drank, his dad was loud, so he became loud. He found that he could bully people into getting his way. As he grew up, he married and began having children. He too continued to drink heavily. So heavily that he too missed work and was often fired. The same line of problems his dad had were now identically in his life. Finally, one day the younger son went to church and heard enough of the gospel to know that he needed to "get saved".

Even though he knew he was serious when he went down the aisle, he couldn't seem to stop drinking and gambling. Then one Sunday he found what he thought was the solution. He heard about generational curses.

Immediately he thought, "That was it! This situation isn't my fault; it's my dad's. I'm under a curse!" If I can go back and find the reason why my dad did these things, I can be free.

The self-trained "professional" counselor was more than happy to take on the young man's case. With all his problems, she was sure that this would be a long-term in-depth process of searching through all the family ancestry, and she was right. Rather than looking to Jesus and believing what God's word said, the young man continuously kept looking at himself and his dad's sins.

Instead of freedom, the young man simply learned how to hide his problems. Instead of ever reaching the level of freedom Jesus died to provide, the young man adopted a theology that said, he wasn't supposed to prosper. The reality was if the young man had simply not continued his father's practices, he would have moved out of the poverty mindset and would have prospered.

You see the problem wasn't the man's past or his father's past; it was the young man's present. He never moved into the present day lordship of Jesus. Instead he continued practicing his father's sin practices and it brought destruction. There are many aspects of sowing and reaping. As I said earlier most problems stem back to this.

Unfortunately, many people that are still broken and wounded in their own hearts have found a way to be needed by becoming a purveyor of the various counseling theologies. Many people that are "ministering" have themselves never been healed. Many have a need to be needed. Some have a need to be seen as an expert at something because this in itself feeds their lack of self-esteem or has become their identity rather than accepting the identity that Christ has for them.

When people can't win, they often change the rules.

There is nothing in the Word of God telling us to try to counsel people into the image of Christ. We are told to go into all the world and make disciples, not clients or patients.

The only true way to be free is to find your identity in Christ. You must accept what He has said about who you are and not concern yourself with what people think of you.

The scriptures are clear. Sow to the flesh – reap corruption. Sow to the spirit – reap life everlasting. Every minute you spend doing carnal things to try to meet spiritual needs, you are sowing to the flesh. It will never meet the cry of your heart. Find out who you truly are.

Delve into the apostle Paul's writings concerning the new man. Find out who God re-created you to be on the inside. Then let it out to be seen by others on the outside.

Accidents:

I am not going to spend much time on this area, but it is important to see the truth that it brings forth. There are some that would say that there is no such thing as an accident. This is an area where we would have to come to an agreement on definitions or terminology.

When I say "accident", I mean it wasn't "planned". Someone might argue that perhaps satan had planned it. That could be true, and if it is then this should be under the next heading of "Attacks".

When I use the term "accidents", as I've said, I simply mean that it wasn't planned by God or humans.
Everything that happens wasn't "planned' by God. He knows everything that will happen, but that doesn't mean that He planned it or that it was His will.

If He planned everything that happens or if everything that happens is His will, then His will is always done and we know that's not true because the word of God tells us that it is not His will that any should perish, but we also know that many perish.

2 Peter 3:9-10
9 The Lord is not slack concerning his promise, as some men count slackness; but is longsuffering to us-ward, not willing that any should perish, but that all should come to repentance.
10 But the day of the Lord will come as a thief in the night; in the which the heavens shall pass away with a great noise, and the elements shall melt with fervent heat, the earth also and the works that are therein shall be burned up. KJV

So, God's will is not always automatically done. Jesus also proves this when He told us to pray, "Thy will be done in earth as it is in heaven".

Matthew 6:10
Thy kingdom come. Thy will be done in earth, as it is in heaven. KJV

If we are to pray that His will be done then it shows that His will is not automatically done. If He told us to pray that way even though His will was going to be done anyway, then He would be guilty of telling us to pray vain prayers of repetitious words. That is a practice He specifically condemned.

Matthew 6:7
But when ye pray, use not vain repetitions, as the heathen do: for they think that they shall be heard for their much speaking. KJV

For a better understanding of this and a more in-depth study, see my teachings concerning: "The Sovereignty of God', "The Truth About Judgment", and "Does God Determine When You Die?"

If everything that happens is indeed the predetermined will of God, then the idea that God turns things around is wrong. Things can't be turned around if everything is God's will and everything is working the way it is supposed to be. It would not be turning it around it would be already heading in the predetermined direction.

Humans repenting wouldn't even be true repentance, it would simply be them being on the path God has predetermined. This would also mean that God is truly responsible for every evil thing that happens because if everything that happens is God's will, so is the evil that happens.

The truth here is simple: Things happen because we live in a fallen and degrading world. When things happen, the enemy can take advantage of them to try to work them in his favor.

God can also take advantage of the things that happen and turn them to His advantage and the advantage of His people and kingdom. He can even show His people things that are going to happen so that they can be ready to act. The problem is that few of His people actually asking Him about things to come.

John 16:13 - Howbeit when he, the Spirit of truth, is come, he will guide you into all truth: for he shall not speak of himself; but whatsoever he shall hear, that shall he speak: and he will shew you things to come. KJV

Attacks:
This is the area where we can take advantage of the power and authority God has given us.

Many Christians believe that God is doing everything that happens. Because of this belief, they are passive about everything that happens. If they get sick, they think it is God trying to teach them something, or He is punishing them for something. As I said, this kind of thinking leads to a passive acceptance (and sometimes even an active pursuit) of problems.

We need to make sure our understanding is one that the Bible promotes. In the early days of the church, Christians knew and understood that problems would come.

Jesus told us that in:

John 16:33
These things I have spoken unto you, that in me <u>ye might have peace</u>. In the world <u>ye shall have tribulation</u>: but be of good cheer; I have overcome the world. KJV
They knew things would happen. They knew persecution would come. They didn't "believe for it". But they knew it would come. Because of that knowing, they knew what to do when it came. STAND!

When we are told today that everything should be perfect and that we should never have problems, we are shaken when things do happen and problems do arise. The Bible is very clear in these things. We are told that we will suffer. We are also told WHAT we will suffer and what we should NOT suffer. For example:

Acts 9:15-16
15 But the Lord said unto him, Go thy way: for he is a chosen vessel unto me, to bear my name before the Gentiles, and kings, and the children of Israel:

16 For I will shew him how great things he must suffer for my name's sake. KJV

God told Paul what he would suffer because of his service. Paul later detailed what he suffered for the cause of Christ:

2 Corinthians 11:23-30
23 Are they ministers of Christ? (I speak as a fool) I am more; in labours more abundant, in stripes above measure, in prisons more frequent, in deaths oft.
24 Of the Jews five times received I forty stripes save one.
25 Thrice was I beaten with rods, once was I stoned, thrice I suffered shipwreck, a night and a day I have been in the deep;
26 In journeyings often, in perils of waters, in perils of robbers, in perils by mine own countrymen, in perils by the heathen, in perils in the city, in perils in the wilderness, in perils in the sea, in perils among false brethren;
27 In weariness and painfulness, in watchings often, in hunger and thirst, in fastings often, in cold and nakedness.
28 Beside those things that are without, that which cometh upon me daily, the care of all the churches.

29 Who is weak, and I am not weak? who is offended, and I burn not?
30 If I must needs glory, I will glory of the things which concern mine infirmities. KJV

All of these things were what Paul suffered. If you look at the lives of the other apostles, you will see that they too suffered similar problems.

Notice that in all the "sufferings" Paul listed, he never mentioned sickness, disease or generational curses. He even said in verse 30 that this list was his list of "infirmities", again proving that his infirmity in the flesh was not sickness but the physical hardships and problems he suffered. This is why he told Timothy, his protégé to suffer hardness as a good soldier of Jesus Christ. (2 Timothy 2:3)

Go through the list of what Paul was telling him. People were saying he was too young. Paul said not to pay attention to what people might say about you. Just live right. Be an example. Then Paul said that he suffered because of how people perceived him. (2 Timothy 2:9)

Again, notice that a lot of his sufferings had to do with persecutions. And what did Jesus say about persecution?

Matthew 5:10
Blessed are they which are persecuted for righteousness' sake: for theirs is the kingdom of heaven. KJV

John 15:20-21
20 Remember the word that I said unto you, The servant is not greater than his lord. If they have persecuted me, <u>they will also persecute you</u>; if they have kept my saying, they will keep yours also.
21 <u>But all these things will they do unto you for my name's sake</u>, because they know not him that sent me. KJV

Notice here that Jesus said they would do all these things FOR MY NAME'S SAKE. The exact same words used when Jesus told Ananias about what Paul would suffer.

Paul even reminded us of this fact in:

2 Corinthians 4:8-9
8 We are troubled on every side, yet not distressed; we are perplexed, but not in despair;
9 Persecuted, but not forsaken; cast down, but not destroyed; KJV

and

2 Timothy 3:12
Yea, and all that will live godly in Christ Jesus shall suffer persecution. KJV

The enemy attacks because he is an enemy of God and man. We must be wise and know his tactics, so that we will not be defeated in any confrontation we may have with him.

Here is what we know and can be assured of:

John 16:33
These things I have spoken unto you, that in me ye might have peace. In the world ye shall have tribulation: but be of good cheer; I have overcome the world. KJV

1 John 2:13-14
13 I write unto you, fathers, because ye have known him that is from the beginning. I write unto you, young men, because ye have <u>overcome the wicked one</u>. I write unto you, little children, because ye have known the Father.
14 I have written unto you, fathers, because ye have known him that is from the beginning. I have written unto you, young men, because ye are strong, and the word of God abideth in you, and <u>ye have overcome the wicked one</u>. KJV

Romans 12:21
Be not overcome of evil, but <u>overcome evil with good</u>.
KJV

1 Corinthians 15:57
But thanks be to God, which <u>giveth us the victory</u> through our Lord Jesus Christ.

1 John 5:4-5
4 For whatsoever is born of God <u>overcometh</u> the world: and <u>this is the victory that overcometh the world, even our faith.</u>
5 Who is he that <u>overcometh the world</u>, but he that believeth that Jesus is the Son of God? KJV

2 Corinthians 2:14
Now thanks be unto God, which always <u>causeth us to triumph</u> in Christ, and maketh manifest the savour of his knowledge by us in every place. KJV

We can be victorious EVERY time. It does not say we will not have problems. It says we can be victorious over them EVERY time. We are expected to be victorious EVERY time. We are to walk worthy of the Lord.

Where Do These Problems Come From?

Ephesians 4:1-2
1 I therefore, the prisoner of the Lord, beseech you that ye walk worthy of the vocation wherewith ye are called,
2 With all lowliness and meekness, with longsuffering, forbearing one another in love; KJV

Colossians 1:9-14
9 For this cause we also, since the day we heard it, do not cease to pray for you, and to desire that ye might be filled with the knowledge of his will in all wisdom and spiritual understanding;
10 <u>That ye might walk worthy of the Lord unto all pleasing</u>, being fruitful in every good work, and increasing in the knowledge of God;
11 <u>Strengthened with all might</u>, according to his glorious power, unto all patience and longsuffering with joyfulness;
12 Giving thanks unto the Father, which hath made us meet to be partakers of the inheritance of the saints in light:
13 Who hath delivered us from the power of darkness, and hath translated us into the kingdom of his dear Son:
14 <u>In whom we have redemption through his blood, even the forgiveness of sins</u>: KJV

1 Thessalonians 2:11-13
11 As ye know how we exhorted and comforted and charged every one of you, as a father doth his children,
12 That ye would walk worthy of God, who hath <u>called you unto his kingdom and glory</u>.
13 For this cause also thank we God without ceasing, because, when ye received the word of God which ye heard of us, ye received it not as the word of men, but as it is in truth, the word of God, which effectually worketh also in you that believe. KJV

If you think that every problem you face is to teach you something, or to punish you for something, or is because of some "generational curse", you will never fulfill any of these commands. You will never stand up to the attacker and defeat him. You will never change the behaviors that can make you susceptible to the attacks of the enemy.

So, what is the answer?

We will look at that in the next chapter.

Where Do These Problems Come From?

Chapter 4:
What Do I Do Now?

The answer is simple:

Believe the Bible.

If you are not born-again, get born-again.

Make Jesus Christ your Lord.

If you are born-again, believe the Bible.

Choose to believe what the Bible says about you.

Choose to change the behaviors that have been causing you some of the problems you've experienced.

Choose to stand against the enemy. Do not believe his lies.

Believe that you are a new creation.

Believe that ALL the old things ARE passed away.

Believe that everything in you (in your spirit) is NEW and that it is ALL of God!.

Then begin to renew your mind to the word of God about who it says YOU ARE! (If you need help renewing your mind, contact me. I have a mind renewal program that causes you to begin thinking with the mind of Christ.

You already HAVE His mind; you might as well use it! (1 Corinthians 2:16)

Begin studying the Bible regularly.

Begin speaking it constantly.

Think about it, dwell in it, and meditate on it.

As you read it you will find out what was included in YOUR inheritance!

If this book has been a blessing, then pass it to a friend or start a simple study with a friend. Write me and let me know how it has helped and how I can help you walk into your destiny!

- You are left unsatisfied by the status quo...
- You know you were meant to be a participant and not just a spectator...
- You ask "Why not?..." more than "Why?"...
- You believe that today can be better than yesterday...
- You know you were meant to walk among the Giants of the Faith, and you want the tools & training that can make it happen...
- When you hear the exploits of God's Generals, you can picture yourself doing them...

If this describes you, then you ARE JGLM... whether you know it or not.

COME.
LET'S CHANGE THE WORLD.

John G. Lake Ministries
SAME MESSAGE. SAME POWER. SAME RESULTS.

LIFE TEAM
The Saints Army
lifeteams@jglm.org

Go out into all the world. Preach the gospel, heal the sick, cast out demons and make disciples

John G. Lake Ministries
SAME MESSAGE. SAME POWER. SAME RESULTS.

PARTNER WITH US AS WE ADVANCE GOD'S KINGDOM ON EARTH!

Partner Benefits Include:

- Our monthly "Laboring Together" newsletter with a ministry update directly from Brother Curry that includes detailed information about our upcoming events and activities. We compile testimonies from all over the world to encourage and strengthen your faith.

- Partner E-Newsletter includes an MP3 every month taught by Brother Curry with the option to download our monthly audio teaching.

- 30% Discount on all products during the holiday season...

- Our Promise to Protect Your Kingdom Investment.

Partners can choose to receive packets by postal mail or via email. Your faithful support allows us to help give our materials away freely to those who cannot give, such as our JGLM prison ministries, disaster relief funds and foreign missionaries. Most importantly we depend on our faithful partners as our main line of prayer support.

Email: partners@jglm.org
www.jglm.org/partners

The Teaching That Birthed A Legend Is Now Raising An Army.

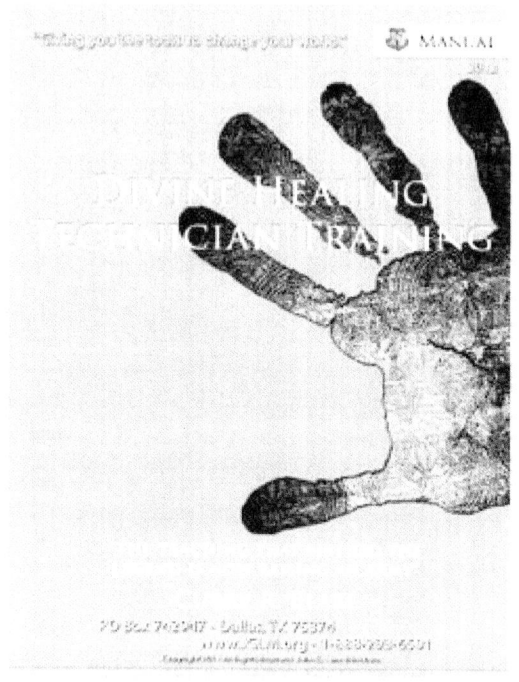

Get Yours Today
Call **888-293-6591**
or Visit Us Online

store.jglm.org

John G. Lake Ministries
SAME MESSAGE. SAME POWER. SAME RESULTS.

DOMINION LIFE

Glory to God, Freedom for All!

Join us online every Sunday at 10am:
broadcast.jglm.org
To learn more about Dominion Life visit:
jglm.org/dominion-life-church
or email: dliac@jglm.org

Church Membership Requirements

1. Must confess Jesus as Lord and that you are saved and born again.

2. Must at least be seeking and expecting to be filled with the Holy Spirit in accordance with Acts Chapter 2 (speaking with other tongues).

3. Must agree with the JGLM/IAC Statement of Faith, obtained by emailing us at: dliac@jglm.org.

4. You agree to pray for us according to the prayer directives that we will send to all church members on a regular basis.

5. You agree to support the church through tithes and offerings. Tithes and offerings must be sent to the church address and MUST be noted as Tithes/Offerings.

6. You agree to work towards becoming a certified DHT. Our hope is that ALL DLIAC members work toward becoming a certified DHT to advance the kingdom through this body. For information on becoming a DHT contact us by email at: iac@jglm.org or you can find all information on our website at www.jglm.org.

7. You agree to remain in the unity of the Spirit by living a life in accordance with the constitution and bylaws of the I.A.C.

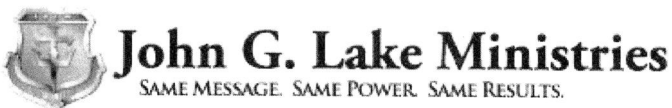

John G. Lake Ministries
SAME MESSAGE. SAME POWER. SAME RESULTS.